Juvenile Accountability Block Grants Program

2008–2009 Report to Congress

Jeff Slowikowski, Acting Administrator
Office of Juvenile Justice and Delinquency Prevention

March 2011

NCJ 231990

Foreword

I am pleased to present the *Juvenile Accountability Block Grants (JABG) Program: 2008–2009 Report to Congress*. This report highlights the accomplishments of the states, territories, local jurisdictions, and American Indian/Alaska Native communities in implemented programs that hold juvenile offenders accountable for their delinquent behavior and promote accountability within juvenile courts and the justice system.

This *JABG Report to Congress* presents data from local subgrantees on how their accountability programs performed during the 2008 and 2009 reporting periods. This report presents the results from the fifth and sixth rounds of performance measurement data collected from U.S. states and territories and the first round of data collected from the tribes. We are encouraged by what the performance data reveal. States, communities, and tribes have embraced the performance measurement initiative; all 56 states and territories provided complete or partial 2008 and 2009 performance data to the Office of Juvenile Justice and Delinquency Prevention (OJJDP), and 51 completed all of their reporting requirements. The data show that grantees are using their JABG funds to make a difference in the specific outcomes that OJJDP and the Office of Justice Programs deem important.

The performance data provide a useful tool to help local jurisdictions, states, and tribes better manage programs, allocate resources, conduct strategic planning, and inform their decisionmaking. States can compare performance across their subgrantees to identify strong programs that might be suitable for rigorous evaluations and from which they may gain important insights into how and why programs succeed. States can also use the data to identify weaker programs that might benefit from targeted training and technical assistance or from a redesign of their approach.

In addition to providing an analysis of the performance measurement data, this report outlines accomplishments at the local and tribal levels, highlights OJJDP's JABG training and technical assistance efforts, and presents results from the Tribal Juvenile Accountability Discretionary Grants program.

Holding youth accountable for their delinquent acts is a matter of basic justice. It combats delinquency and improves the quality of life in our communities. OJJDP looks forward to continuing partnerships with stakeholders at the federal, state, local, and tribal levels to ensure that all youth benefit from an accountability-based approach to juvenile justice.

Jeff Slowikowski
Acting Administrator
Office of Juvenile Justice and Delinquency Prevention

Table of Contents

List of Exhibits

Chapter 1: Introduction to OJJDP's Juvenile Accountability Block Grants Program

The Juvenile Accountability Block Grants (JABG) program provides funds to states[1] to support programs that promote accountability for juvenile offenders and systems. The JABG program is based on research studies of youth and juvenile offenders that have demonstrated that applying consequences or sanctions swiftly, consistently, and in a graduated manner commensurate with the severity of the offense and the offender's prior criminal history works best in preventing, controlling, and reducing the likelihood of subsequent violations.

For the offender, accountability means holding a juvenile who has violated the law (by admission or adjudication) responsible for the behavior by imposing individualized consequences (or sanctions) proportionate to the offense. These sanctions can include restitution, community service, victim-offender mediation, intensive supervision, house arrest, or confinement. The goal is to make the youth aware of the loss, damage, or injury that the victim experiences and to hold him or her responsible. For the juvenile justice system, accountability means increasing the capacity to enhance youth competence, to efficiently track juveniles through the system, and to provide options such as restitution, community service, victim-offender mediation, and other restorative justice sanctions.

The long-term goals of the JABG program are as follows:

♦ By 2014, 78 percent of youth served under the JABG program will be processed using graduated sanctions. (The baseline is 71 percent. The annual goal is a 1-percent increase.)

♦ By 2014, no more than 28 percent of youth served under the JABG program will re-offend. (No baseline is currently available. This rate is based on research of other intervention programs. The annual goal is a 1-percent decrease in rates of offending.)

This report to Congress provides:

♦ An overview and analysis of the fifth and sixth rounds of performance data (for the 2008 and 2009 reporting cycles).

♦ Thumbnail sketches of how the states use their JABG funds.

♦ A description of activities under the Tribal Juvenile Accountability Discretionary Grants program.

♦ Details on the Office of Juvenile Justice and Delinquency Prevention's (OJJDP's) active support for the program.

How the Juvenile Accountability Block Grants Work

Since 1998, OJJDP has helped states and units of local government implement accountability-based programs through the JABG program. The JABG program awards federal formula/block grants to the states and works to encourage states and units of local government to implement accountability-based programs and

---

[1] In the context of this report, the term "states" includes the 50 states, the District of Columbia, and the five territories (American Samoa, Guam, the Northern Mariana Islands, Puerto Rico, and the U.S. Virgin Islands).

services and strengthen the juvenile justice system. States (grantees) must pass 75 percent of these funds through to units of local government. States may apply for a waiver of the passthrough requirement if they demonstrate that they bear the primary financial burden (at least 25 percent) for administering the juvenile justice system.

Congress uses a formula based on the state's juvenile population to determine each state's annual allocation. The Justice Research and Statistics Association (JRSA)[2] calculates local allocations using a formula based on local law enforcement expenditures and the number of local violent crimes reported for the three previous years. States may use the JRSA-generated calculations[3] or conduct their own calculations.

States and subgrantees can spend their JABG funds on programs in the 17 congressionally defined purpose areas listed in exhibit 1. The purpose areas fall under four broad types of activities: hiring staff, training staff, building infrastructure, and implementing programs. OJJDP requires all JABG recipients to assess and report their funded activities annually. How units of local government spent their funds is depicted in exhibit 3 on page 7. The JABG program also provides states and local governments with information about best practices—juvenile justice programs or interventions that research has shown increase juvenile accountability.

Authorizing Legislation

The House of Representatives passed the Juvenile Accountability Incentive Block Grants (JAIBG) Act in 1997 under Title III of H.R. 3. Congress first funded the program through an appropriations act in fiscal year (FY) 1998. OJJDP, as a component of the Office of Justice Programs within the U.S. Department of Justice, is the administering agency. The Department of Justice Authorization Act of FY 2003 included provisions to change the name of the JAIBG program to the Juvenile Accountability Block Grants program, expand the number (from 12 to 16) and scope of the purpose areas, refine the program's reporting and monitoring requirements, and include funding of the program as part of Title I (Part R—Chapter 46—Subchapter XII–F) of the Omnibus Crime Control and Safe Streets Act. Congress added a 17th program area—reentry—in 2006. This report meets the reporting requirements spelled out in the Omnibus Crime Control Act.

In addition to being eligible for JABG funds as a state-designated agency, American Indian tribes, as defined by Section 102 of the Federally Recognized Indian Tribe List Act of 1994 (25 U.S.C. 479a), or a consortia of such tribes, are eligible for JABG funding through OJJDP's Tribal Juvenile Accountability Discretionary Grants (T–JADG) program. OJJDP awards T–JADG grants on a competitive basis (see chapter 3).

---

[2] The Justice Research and Statistics Association (JRSA) is a national nonprofit organization of state Statistical Analysis Center (SAC) directors, researchers, and practitioners throughout government, academia, and criminal justice organizations. Created in 1974, JRSA promotes the exchange of information among the SACs, enabling them to work toward common goals, and serves as a liaison between the state agencies and the Justice Department. JRSA is supported through grants from the Bureau of Justice Statistics.

[3] About 90 percent of states use these calculations.

Exhibit 1: JABG Purpose Areas

The goal of the Juvenile Accountability Block Grants (JABG) program is to reduce juvenile offending through accountability-based programs focused on juvenile offenders and the juvenile justice system. To meet that goal and strengthen the juvenile justice system, a state or unit of local government may use JABG funds to perform the following activities:

1. Developing, implementing, and administering graduated sanctions for juvenile offenders.

2. Building, expanding, renovating, or operating temporary or permanent juvenile corrections, juvenile detention, or community corrections facilities.

3. Hiring juvenile court judges, probation officers, court-appointed defenders, and special advocates and funding pretrial services for juvenile offenders to promote the effective and expeditious administration of the juvenile justice system.

4. Hiring additional prosecutors so that more cases involving violent juvenile offenders can be prosecuted and case backlogs can be reduced.

5. Providing funding to enable prosecutors to address drug, gang, and youth violence problems more effectively. Providing funding for technology, equipment, and training to help prosecutors identify and expedite the prosecution of violent juvenile offenders.

6. Establishing and maintaining training programs for law enforcement and other court personnel with respect to preventing and controlling juvenile crime.

7. Establishing juvenile gun courts for the prosecution and adjudication of juvenile firearms offenders.

8. Establishing drug court programs for juvenile offenders that provide continuing judicial supervision over juvenile offenders with substance abuse problems and integrate the administration of other sanctions and services for such offenders.

9. Establishing and maintaining a system of juvenile records designed to promote public safety.

10. Establishing and maintaining interagency information-sharing programs that enable the juvenile and criminal justice systems, schools, and social services agencies to make more informed decisions about the early identification, control, supervision, and treatment of juveniles who repeatedly commit serious delinquent or criminal acts.

11. Establishing and maintaining accountability-based programs designed to reduce recidivism among juveniles who are referred by law enforcement personnel or agencies.

12. Establishing and maintaining programs to conduct risk and needs assessments that facilitate effective early intervention and help provide comprehensive services (including mental health and substance abuse screening and treatment) to juvenile offenders.

13. Establishing and maintaining accountability-based programs that are designed to enhance school safety. These programs may include research-based bullying, cyberbullying, and gang prevention programs.

14. Establishing and maintaining restorative justice programs.

15. Establishing and maintaining programs to enable juvenile courts and juvenile probation officers to be more effective and efficient in holding juvenile offenders accountable and reducing recidivism.

16. Hiring detention and corrections personnel. Establishing and maintaining training programs for such personnel to improve facility practices and programming.

17. Establishing, improving, and coordinating prerelease and postrelease systems and programs to facilitate the successful reentry of juvenile offenders from state and local custody in the community.

Chapter 2: Results From the Fifth and Sixth Collections of JABG Data

In Fiscal Year (FY) 2004, the Office of Juvenile Justice and Delinquency Prevention (OJJDP) began requiring all states and territories receiving Juvenile Accountability Block Grants (JABG) funds to submit annual performance data. JABG was the first OJJDP grant program to implement such extensive, quantitative performance measures. OJJDP provides a menu of approximately 300 output and outcome performance indicators from which grantees can select. The indicator list is organized by the 17 purpose areas (see exhibit 1). States may allocate their program funds under one of the areas listed in the exhibit. OJJDP requires states to submit data for at least one indicator of output performance, one indicator of short-term outcome performance, and one indicator of intermediate outcome performance.

As OJJDP expanded its performance measurement system, the Office developed a list of core measures and began to apply them to all juvenile justice programs.[4] OJJDP also developed mandatory performance indicators to ensure that all grantees report on these core measures. Exhibit 2 shows the mandatory indicators for the JABG program. As shown, OJJDP requires all grantees to report the number and percentage of youth served who reoffend. Requirements for other indicators vary based on whether a program provides direct services to youth and families or uses JABG funds for juvenile justice system improvement.

---

[4] These are the measures that OJJDP reported as part of its 2006 Program Assessment Rating Tool review of Juvenile Justice programs. For more information, go to www.whitehouse.gov/omb/expectmore/summary/10003813.2006.html.

Reporting Cycles and Periods

States and units of local government report their performance data on an annual reporting cycle. A reporting cycle consists of a 12-month reporting period, followed by a 3-month period in which data must be submitted.

To illustrate, grantees and subgrantees collected JABG data during the reporting period April 1, 2007, to March 31, 2008, and submitted it through June 30, 2008.

2008–2009 JABG Results

This section presents the performance data for the fifth and sixth JABG reporting periods, April 1, 2007, to March 31, 2008, and April 1, 2008, to March 31, 2009. The data represent information that states collected from their subgrantees. The final responsibility for the accuracy and validity of these data rests with OJJDP.

Funding

Because JABG grantees have a multiple-year funding period, they do not necessarily spend funds in the calendar year or fiscal year in which their funds are awarded. Thus, the funds a state may award to its subgrantees during a given fiscal year can derive from prior fiscal years. In the 2008 reporting period, the 2,055 subgrants awarded accounted for approximately $154 million and were derived from 6 fiscal years (FY 2003 through FY 2008). In the 2009 reporting period, the 1,462 subgrants awarded accounted for approximately $80 million and were derived from six fiscal years (FY 2004 through FY 2009).

Exhibit 2: Mandatory Performance Indicators for the JABG Program

Indicator Type	Direct-Service Programs	System-Improvement Programs
Output.	Number and percentage of eligible youth served using graduated sanctions approaches.	JABG funds awarded for system improvement (e.g., hiring or training staff or increasing system capacity).
Short-term outcome (outcomes accomplished during program).	Number and percentage of program youth completing program requirements. Number and percentage of program youth who reoffend.	Number and percentage of programs/initiatives employing best practices.
Intermediate-term outcome (outcomes accomplished after initial implementation).	N/A	Number and percentage of eligible youth served using graduated sanctions approaches. Number and percentage of youth with whom a best practice was used.
Long-term outcome (outcomes accomplished 6 to 12 months after program ends).	Number and percentage of program youth who reoffend.	Number and percentage of program youth who reoffend.

OJJDP distributed approximately $42 million in FY 2008 and more than $48 million in FY 2009 under the JABG program. All 50 states, the District of Columbia, and the U.S. territories are eligible for JABG funds.

Performance Measurement

To assess the effectiveness of the JABG program, OJJDP developed a set of performance measures that help the Office, Congress, and the juvenile justice field see the progress and the challenges facing the program. During the 2008–2009 reporting cycles, OJJDP continued to work with the states to collect quantitative performance measurement data.

For the 2008 reporting period, all 56 JABG grantees submitted at least partial performance data. The states submitted information for approximately 1,645 subgrants[5] and reported performance data for 1,528, or 93 percent, of those subgrants. This represents more than $80 million in funded activities. For the 2009

reporting period, all 56 JABG grantees submitted at least partial performance data. The states submitted information about approximately 1,462 subgrants and reported performance data for 1,399, or 96 percent, of those subgrants, which accounted for more than $80 million in funded activities.

During the 2008 and 2009 reporting periods, the JABG grantees and subgrantees reported performance measurement data regarding activities that were funded by active awards between FY 2003 and FY 2009. Funds were allocated to activities across all 17 JABG purpose areas. The

---

[5] This number is an estimate. To expedite reporting, some grantees reported data aggregated across multiple subgrants. In addition, selected subgrantees received grant modifications late in the reporting cycle and reported the additional funds as separate subgrants. The states did not provide performance data for 410 subgrants (20 percent) because they determined that requiring those subgrantees to do so would have imposed an undue burden on them.

activities with the greatest funding allocations included:

♦ Accountability-based programs: 22 percent in 2008 and 25 percent in 2009.

♦ Court and probation programming: 13 percent in 2008 and 16 percent in 2009.

♦ Restorative justice: 10 percent in 2008 and 9 percent in 2009.

A breakdown of how JABG funds were allocated, by purpose area, follows in exhibit 3.

JABG programs served more than 440,000 youth during the 2008 and 2009 reporting periods. The following is a summary of information about the performance of JABG grantees and subgrantees:

♦ Nineteen percent (301 of 1,645) of programs in 2008 and 21 percent (309 of 1,462) of programs in 2009 reported using an evidence-based program or practice.

♦ Sixty-three percent (149,756 of 239,485) of program youth in 2008 and 73 percent (142,101 of 195,257) of program youth in

Exhibit 3: Number of Subgrants per Program Category Between 2008 and 2009

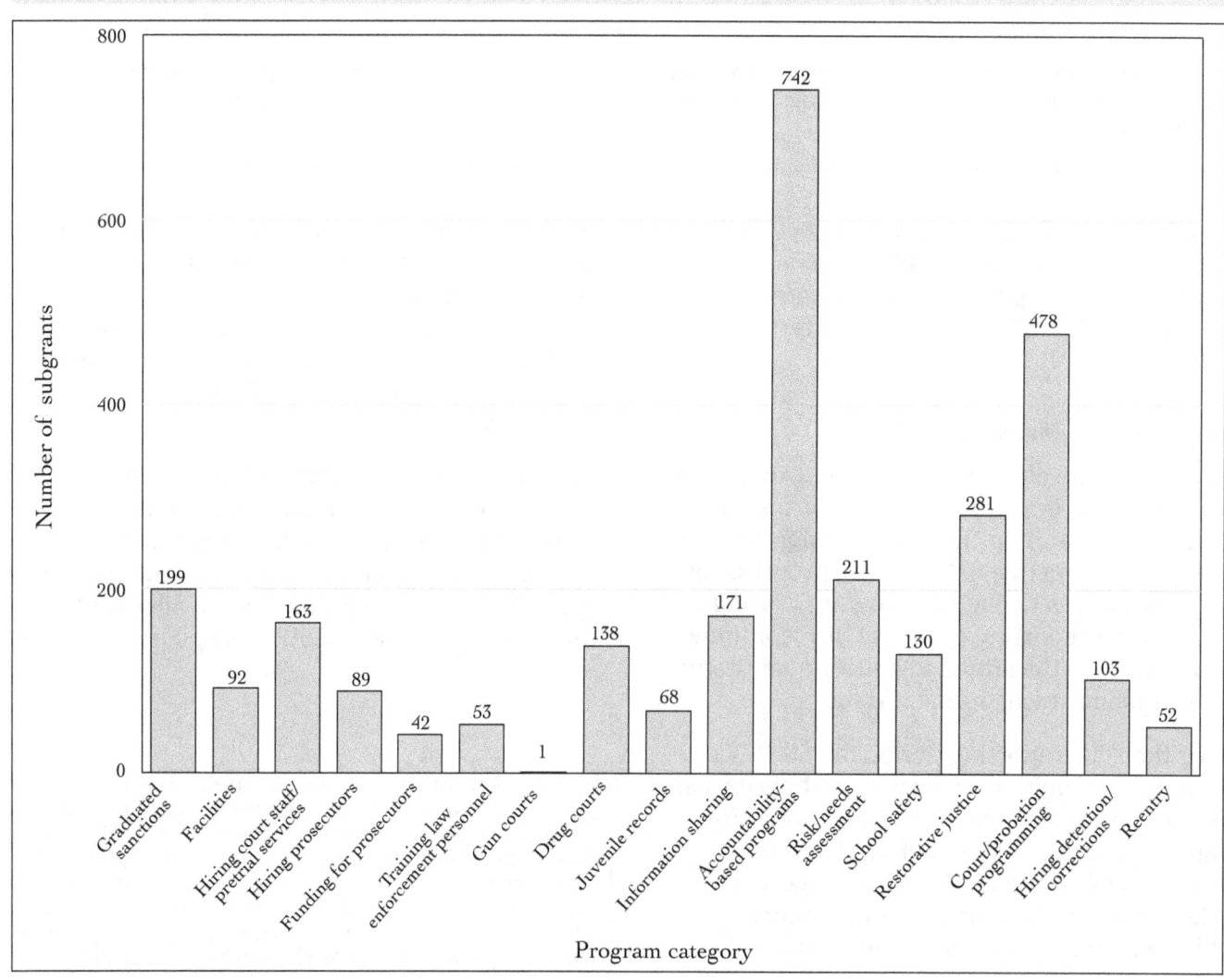

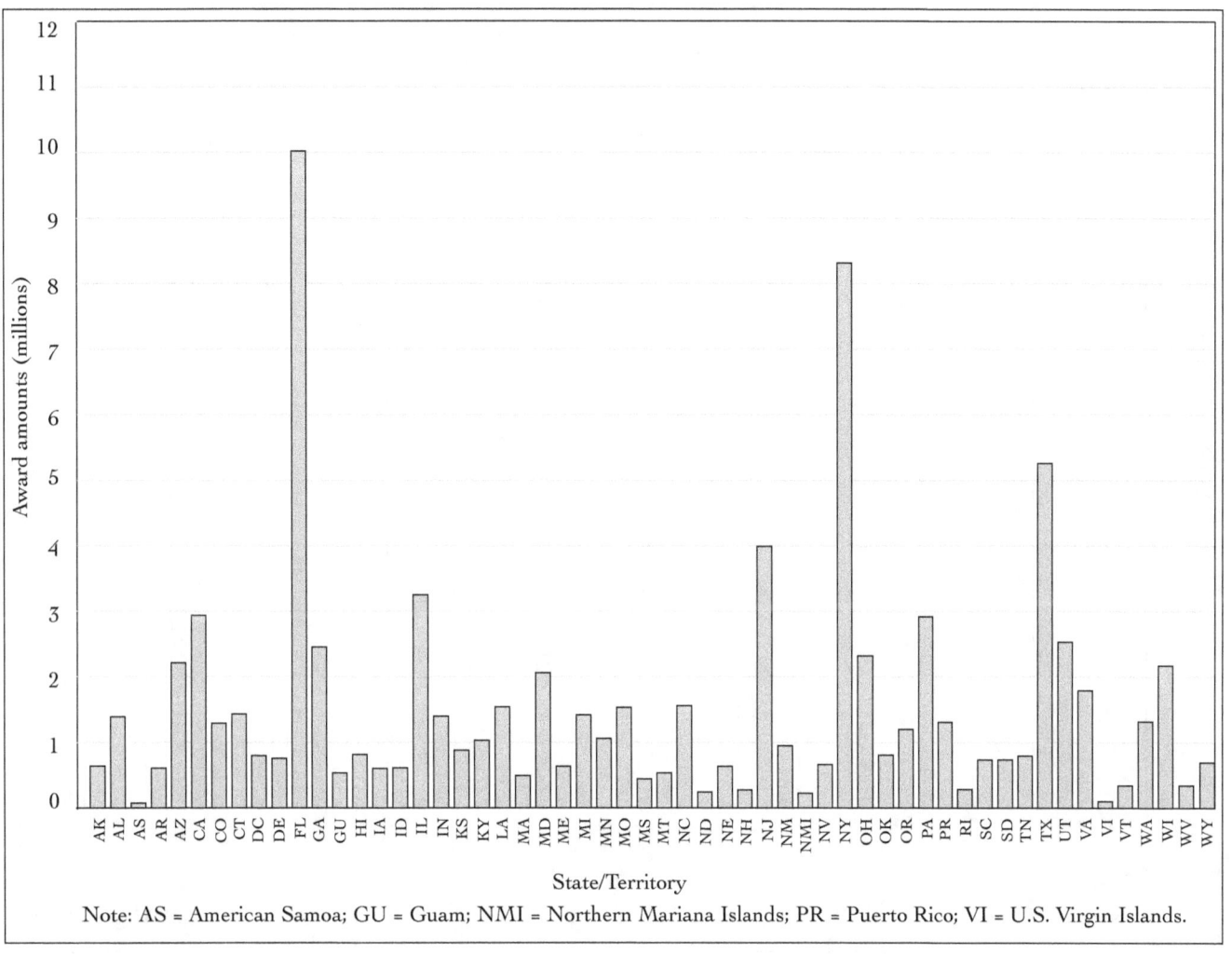

Note: AS = American Samoa; GU = Guam; NMI = Northern Mariana Islands; PR = Puerto Rico; VI = U.S. Virgin Islands.

2009 exhibited a desirable change in targeted behavior.[6]

♦ Seventy-eight percent (152,051 of 196,038) of youth who exited a program in 2008 and 77 percent (99,109 of 128,827) of youth who exited a program in 2009 successfully completed program requirements.

♦ Sixteen percent of program youth reoffended during the program period in 2008, and 20 percent reoffended during the program period in 2009.

When OJJDP analyzed subgrant award amounts by state in 2008, results revealed that Florida awarded the largest amount of funding to its subgrantees. New York and Texas awarded the second and third greatest amounts of funding, respectively, to their subgrantees (see exhibit 4). In 2009, Delaware awarded the largest amount of funding to its subgrantees, followed by Nevada and then Arizona (see exhibit 5).

OJJDP also analyzed data on the types of organizations that implemented the subgrants.

[6] Targeted behaviors differed, depending on the youth's specific program goals. In the majority of cases, JABG programs targeted a reduction in antisocial behavior and improvement in youth's school attendance and social competence.

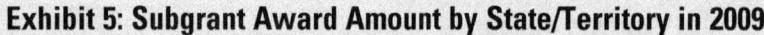

Award amounts (millions)

State/Territory

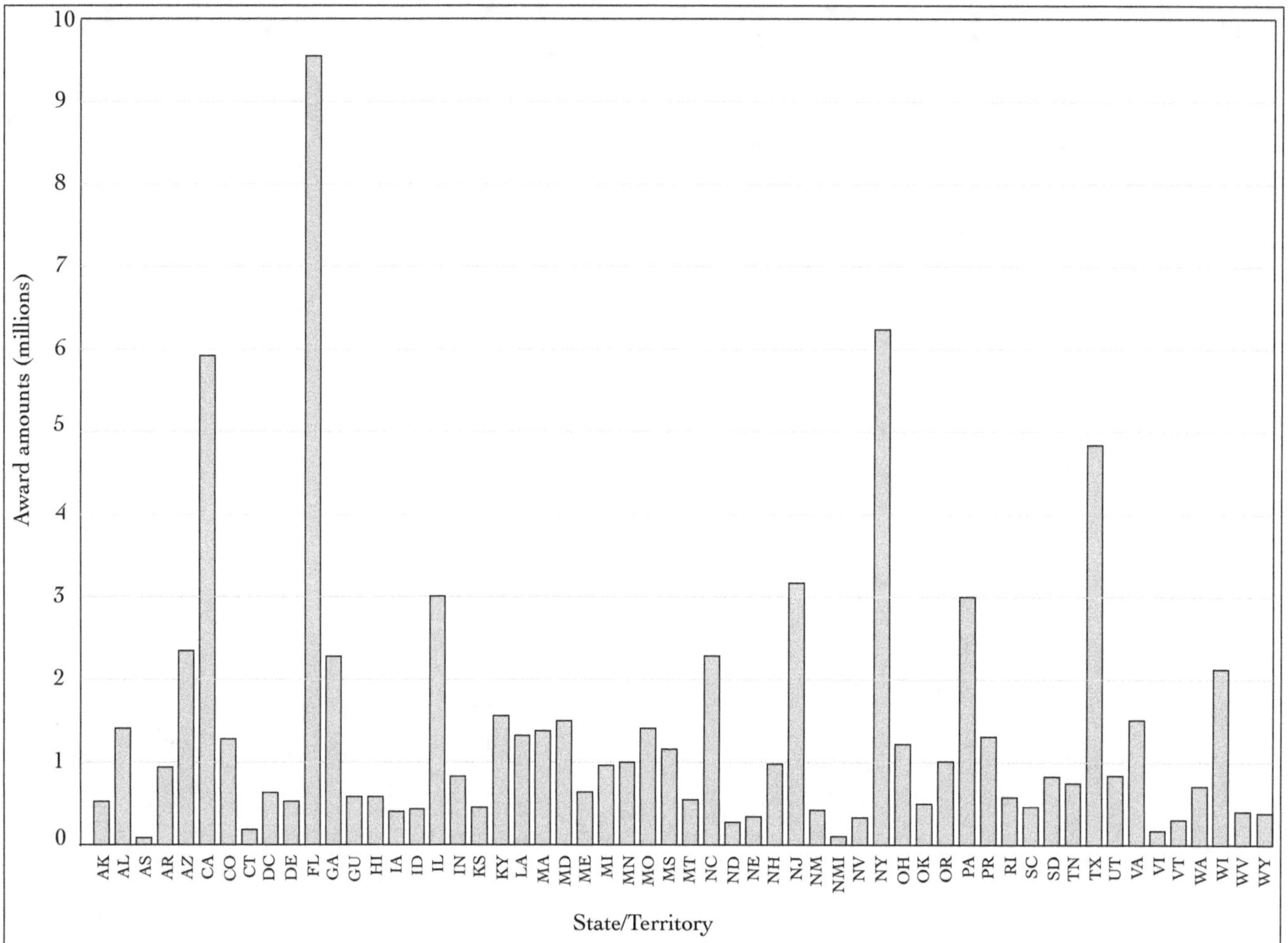

Note: AS = American Samoa; GU = Guam; NMI = Northern Mariana Islands; PR = Puerto Rico; VI = U.S. Virgin Islands.

Results of that analysis follow in exhibit 6. Because this was not a reporting requirement, 830 organizations did not report. Of those organizations that did report, the most common implementing agency was a unit of local government.

OJJDP Support to the Field

OJJDP provides training and technical assistance through a number of providers:

♦ The National Training and Technical Assistance Center (NTTAC) provides telephone or onsite training and technical assistance. The majority of the requests NTTAC received in 2008 for JABG training

and technical assistance were in the areas of corrections/detention facilities, restorative justice, juvenile courts and probation, detention/corrections personnel, training for law enforcement and court personnel, information sharing, and risk and needs assessment. In 2009, NTTAC also received a number of requests for training and technical assistance on graduated sanctions and reentry.

♦ CSR, Inc., manages the Data Collection and Technical Assistance Tool that OJJDP encourages states to use when submitting JABG performance measurement data. CSR staff also provide training and support to

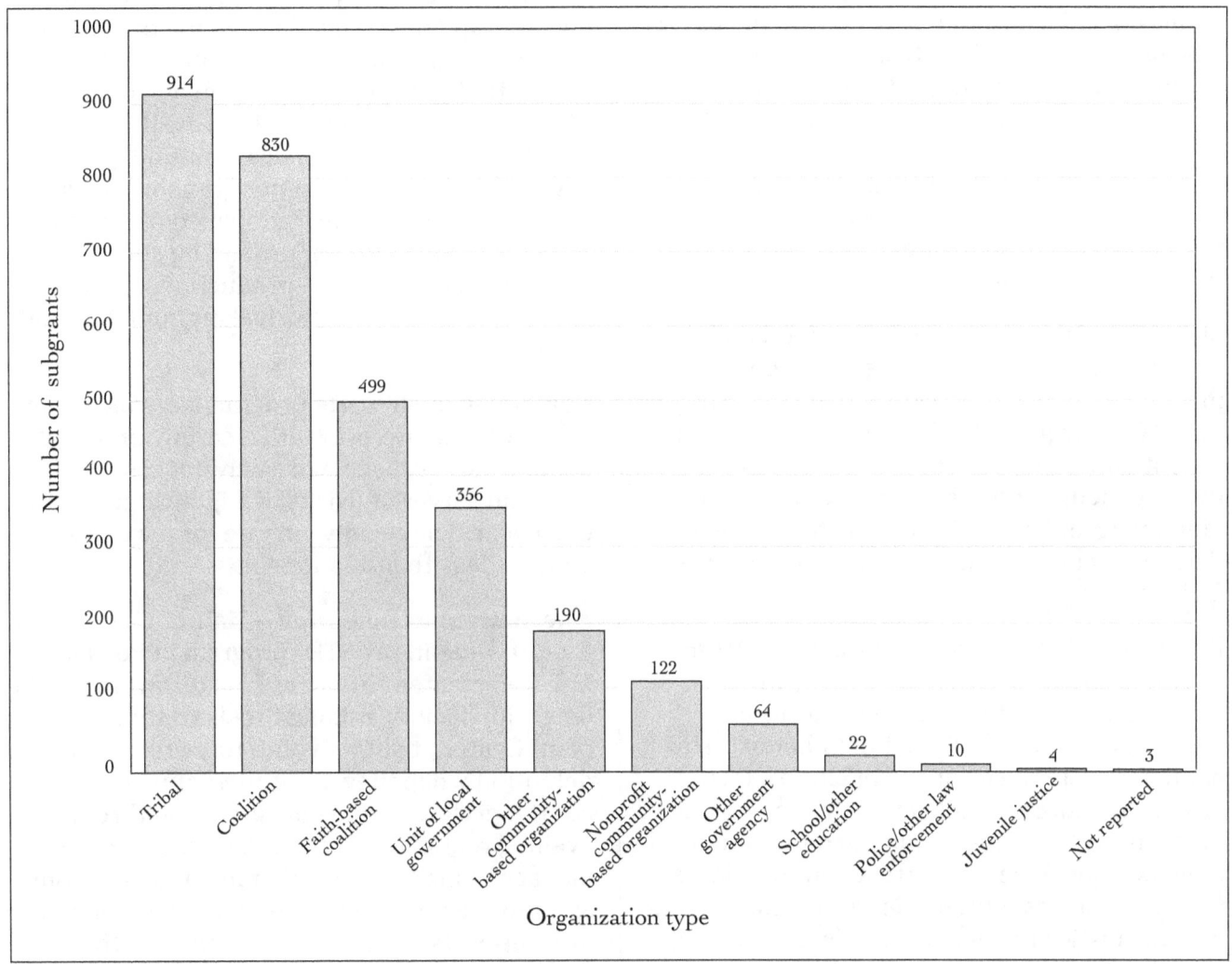

states on the use of the JABG performance measures.

◆ The JABG Technical Assistance Support Center, established by OJJDP with a grant from the Bureau of Justice Statistics to the Justice Research and Statistics Association, provides states the data they need to calculate JABG allocations for local jurisdictions.

During the 2008 JABG reporting period, OJJDP provided 31 JABG training and technical assistance events to 648 individuals from 16 states and the District of Columbia. This support was

in the form of workshops, conference presentations, funding, resource identification, and curriculum development. Recipients included probation officers, substance abuse treatment providers, family advocates, judges, clerks and court staff, juvenile justice residential and detention staff, members of community organizations, and state advisory group members.

During the 2008 reporting period, OJJDP offered the following trainings:

Mental Health Services Delivery for Youth in Detention and Corrections Webinar. This online training was conducted in July 2007,

September 2007, and October 2007 for 348 participants from Florida, North Carolina, Texas, California, Alabama, Kansas, Michigan, and Louisiana. It focused on the elements of delivering effective mental health services to youth in detention and corrections. It addressed common mental health disorders, mental health screening and assessment, how to interact with and respond to youth with mental health disorders, treatment of mental health disorders, collaborations/system integration, and how to develop action plans.

Mental Health Services Delivery for Youth in Detention and Corrections Training. This mental health training event was held in Houston, TX, in August 2007 for 100 juvenile justice practitioners from across the United States. The training focused on assisting practitioners with identifying and assessing mental health disorders of juveniles in detention and corrections facilities.

During the 2009 JABG reporting period, OJJDP provided eight JABG training and technical assistance events to 143 individuals from seven states and the District of Columbia. This support was in the form of workshops, focus groups, resource identification, and curriculum development. Recipients included probation officers, substance abuse treatment providers, family advocates, judges, clerks and court staff, juvenile justice residential and detention staff, members of community organizations, and juvenile justice coalition members. OJJDP offered JABG trainings on topics such as mental health in detention and corrections, law enforcement training, graduated sanctions, reentry, risk and needs assessments, and pretrial services.

Accomplishments at the State and Local Levels

The following descriptions provide a few examples of how OJJDP and the JABG program helped local and state jurisdictions strengthen their juvenile justice systems during the 2008 and 2009 reporting periods.

Sentenced to the Arts Program—Missouri. Jackson and Clay Counties, MO, offer adjudicated youth a variety of art venues and expressive therapy programs through the Sentenced to the Arts program. Youth are matched with an adult artist who engages them in an art interest of their choice. Examples of the available activities include music, ceramics, painting, poetry, sculpting, theater, computer graphics, mural painting, choir, improvisational comedy, model airplane design, African drumming and dance, video and compact disc production, creative writing, piano, varied musical instruments, and modern dance.

Combining quality arts programming based on each youth's interests with a caring, practicing adult artist has been extremely successful. The program serves at least 600 adjudicated youth each year. The recidivism rate for participating youth is less than 15 percent.

Alternatives to Detention—Maine. The Alternatives to Detention (ATD) program in Portland, ME, was created to address overcrowding in the detention facility at Long Creek Youth Development Center. It allows youth to be released from detention while they await their appearance in court. Services include an afternoon-through-evening reporting center and intensive case management. A system of graduated sanctions and rewards provides incentives, and community supports remain in place after youth are discharged from the program.

Combined with other efforts, ATD has contributed to a significant decline in the detention population. From April 2007 through March 2008, the program served 24 youth by using graduated sanctions. Additionally, the program accomplished the following:

♦ Ninety percent of youth leaving the program had successfully completed program requirements.

♦ Only 12.5 percent of youth reoffended while in the program.

◆ Ninety percent of youth who had a goal of finding employment were placed in jobs.

◆ All youth appeared in court as scheduled and did not interfere with the court process.

◆ All participating youth completed 175 hours of service to the community.

Juvenile Accountability Conferences—North Dakota. Juvenile accountability conferences bring together offenders, victims, and key supporters of both with a trained facilitator to discuss the impact of the crime and how to re-pair the harm that has been caused. As part of its restorative justice program, North Dakota's juvenile court has used juvenile accountability conferences statewide as an intervention for misdemeanor offenders and property offenders at all levels. The conferences have increased justice system responsiveness by addressing reparation and accountability for the offend-ers while fulfilling concerns of the victims and communities. Participation in juvenile account-ability conferences is voluntary. Satisfaction surveys—which victims, parents/guardians, and juvenile offenders complete—have shown the following outcomes:

◆ Ninety-five percent of victims stated it was helpful to meet the offender.

◆ Ninety-four percent of victims believed the offender had learned from the process.

◆ Ninety-six percent of parents/guardians of the offender believed their child had learned something from the process.

◆ Ninety-six percent of juvenile offenders believed they had learned something

that could prevent a similar incident from occurring.

◆ Eighty-four percent of juvenile offenders believed that it was helpful to meet the victim.

The JABG Program for Genesee County's Family Division—Michigan. The JABG Program for Genesee County's Family Division of the 7th Judicial Circuit Court focuses on juvenile sub-stance abusers and their families. Two trained probation officers, whose salaries are partially paid by JABG funds, manage a caseload of as many as 20 juveniles who have substance abuse problems and/or gun charges. Numerous orga-nizations work with the probation officers to en-sure program success for the juvenile offenders.

The drug court has several options—such as electronic monitoring, psychological evalu-ations, and mental health assessments—to address the needs of participating juvenile drug offenders. The staff also have been trained to use a breathalyzer and have ready access to one. Drug court probation officers' duties include intensive supervision of participating youth, random drug screenings, and transport-ing clients and parents to and from treatment programs. The drug court was used primarily as a support and intervention program to coincide with the JABG program, and the weekly con-tacts with the court have been effective in modi-fying participating youth's behavior. Graduated sanctions and rewards were built into the pro-bation contract to provide incentives for youth to improve their behavior and to comply with the program.

Chapter 3: Tribal Juvenile Accountability Discretionary Grants Program

The Tribal Juvenile Accountability Discretionary Grants program (T–JADG) funds programs that hold American Indian/Alaska Native (AI/AN) youth accountable for their offenses and provide the necessary resources and support for positive outcomes and reduced recidivism. T–JADG funds are a separate allocation within the Juvenile Accountability Block Grants (JABG) appropriation. The Office of Juvenile Justice and Delinquency Prevention (OJJDP) administers the T–JADG program through its Tribal Youth program. OJJDP awards T–JADG cooperative agreements to federally recognized tribes through a competitive process.

In FY 2008, OJJDP awarded T–JADG grants— a total of more than $1 million—to three tribes. Brief descriptions of the 2008 T–JADG grantees follow.

Coquille Indian Tribe. Located in North Bend, OR, next to Coos Bay, this tribe has used its T–JADG grant to foster connections with neighboring counties and inform them about its Peacegiving Court, a tribal court that serves as an alternative to state jurisdiction for resolving cases involving tribal members. The court has tried 17 cases since its founding in 2005, and most of them have involved tribal youth. Over the past year, the tribe has developed agreements with the courts, district attorneys' offices, social services, school districts, and law enforcement agencies in five neighboring counties. Court staff collaborate with these counties on individual cases.

The goal of the court is to allow cases involving enrolled tribal members who live off the reservation in the five counties to have their cases heard. The tribe uses a video and PowerPoint presentation in its outreach to the five counties, and court staff work with the tribal members in the counties to build a consensus that the Peacegiving Court is a viable alternative to state courts. The grant has also enabled the tribe to create a data management system for court documents, which will be essential for evaluating the court's services.

Court staff will continue to educate tribal members in other counties about their legal rights and opportunities. The tribe hopes that members of surrounding communities will embrace the Peacegiving Court and use it as a model to address juvenile justice throughout Indian country.

Chippewa Cree Tribe. This tribe, based in north central Montana, proposes to develop an accountability-based program—the Rocky Boy's Children's Court Enhancement Project— within the Chippewa Cree tribal court. The project expects to serve 80 juveniles (ages 12 to 17) per year, or a total of 240 juveniles over the 3-year project period. The project will establish accountability-based programs to reduce recidivism among juvenile offenders, provide assessment and screening, and facilitate evidence-based programming, case management, and compliance oversight.

Fallon Paiute Shoshone Tribe. The Fallon Indian Reservation and Colony in west central Nevada will establish and implement a juvenile court to serve 298 Fallon Paiute Shoshone youth ages 8 to 17. The Fallon tribal juvenile court will allow the judicial system to focus exclusively on juvenile delinquency issues, most of which are currently handled through the adult Fallon tribal court. The adult court handles a large volume of adult cases, and the juvenile cases/issues are given lower priority than other criminal matters (such as arraignments or bench and jury trials). The new juvenile court will allow the tribe to establish a separate forum with designated personnel (judge, clerk, prosecutor, probation, defense advocate) to process juvenile cases more effectively and provide greater accountability and supervision of juvenile offenders. The juvenile court also will establish a series of training programs on juvenile delinquency for court and police personnel.

In Fiscal Year (FY) 2009, OJJDP awarded T–JADG grants—a total of more than $2.1 million—to seven tribes. Brief descriptions of the FY 2009 T–JADG grantees follow.

Menominee Indian Tribe of Wisconsin. The tribe will use its T–JADG funds to establish an accountability-based restorative justice program. The tribe will serve 563 youth (ages 11 to 17) who have been identified as truant. The project will develop a Menominee teen court to provide support services to habitually truant youth and youth exhibiting minor behavior problems. The goal of the project is to reduce truancy rates, recidivism, and school incident reports among participating youth.

Red Cliff Band of Lake Superior Chippewa. The Red Cliff Reservation is located at the tip of the Bayfield peninsula in northern Wisconsin. Using grant funds, the tribe will hire a youth officer to follow up on truancy and petty crime cases, improve the collection of juvenile records for tribal and county data, and establish restorative and accountability-based justice programs. Participating juvenile offenders will receive cognitive behavioral therapy that will emphasize taking personal responsibility for their actions through public apologies and dedicated community service. The tribe expects to serve 15 to 25 youth (ages 12 to 17) per year.

Mississippi Band of Choctaw Indians. The Mississippi Band of Choctaw Indians, located in east central Mississippi, will use its T–JADG

funds to establish a juvenile drug court. Of the total tribal population of 9,527, approximately 4,300 (45 percent) are children younger than 18 years old. Almost all members live on or near the tribe's reservation. The reservation is "dry," yet alcohol consumption and substance abuse are commonplace among tribal youth, and intoxication is one of the most prevalent juvenile offenses. The tribal drug court will target juveniles ages 13 to 17. The program would serve 12 participants per year, or 36 youth over the 3-year program period. The project goal is to operate a sentencing diversion for juvenile alcohol and substance offenders, which would further strengthen the existing tribal court. The supporting objectives are as follows:

♦ **Reduce youth offender recidivism.** The program will reduce criminal activity that occurs as a result of substance and alcohol abuse and ensure that 75 percent of participants complete the program successfully.

♦ **Help families.** The program will provide support, instruction, and education to promote healthy families. Its design incorporates the drug court model, the group therapy matrix model, Alcoholics Anonymous (12-step meetings), individual counseling and therapy, family involvement, and outdoor therapeutic activities.

Omaha Tribe of Nebraska. The tribe is located in rural northeastern Nebraska. The tribe's juvenile justice system is chronically underfunded, resulting in insufficient law enforcement coverage, inadequate records and data management systems, limited access to training for law enforcement and justice personnel, and a shortage of comprehensive diversion and sanctions programs. The program hopes to serve 150 juveniles (ages 7 to 14) through a juvenile court system over the course of the grant period.

The program's goals are to develop a comprehensive strategic plan and design a coordinated juvenile justice service system that enhances and adds to existing services. The tribe will establish an advisory board to oversee the plan, revise tribal codes to identify and address challenges facing juvenile offenders, integrate treatment for youth offenders and families, and provide a culturally appropriate, family-based prevention and intervention system to address delinquency on the reservation. The program will focus on risk factors that include gang membership, truancy, and violence; increase the number of youth directly served by prevention programs; and implement collaborative intervention alternatives.

Reno-Sparks Indian Colony. The Reno-Sparks Indian Colony is located in Hungry Valley, Nevada. The tribe will develop an accountability-based juvenile justice system to address truancy and delinquent behavior among tribal youth. The tribal court will target 50 youth (younger than 17 years old) out of a possible 305 youth who are eligible. The court will conduct an outcome evaluation as part of an effort to improve the quality and integrity of the program. The court will develop a teen or peer court and involve juvenile offenders in the community. Juvenile probation officers will provide guidance and involve adjudicated juvenile offenders in community building and other positive activities. The court will assess offender outcomes throughout their participation in the program (at intake, at completion, and at 6 months of followup). The outcome evaluation will focus on the degree to which the juvenile offender has changed at-risk behaviors in a way that can be attributed to program services.

Northern Cheyenne Tribe. The Northern Cheyenne Indian Reservation is located in rural southeastern Montana near the town of Lame Deer. The tribe proposes to unify local law enforcement, substance abuse, criminal justice, and social service agencies to control and prevent crime, truancy, school dropouts, substance abuse, and associated problems. The goal of this program is to reduce juvenile offending through accountability-based programs focused on 25 to 40 juvenile offenders, (ages 12 to 17). To this end, the Northern Cheyenne court will develop, implement, and administer graduated sanctions for juvenile offenders; hire juvenile court judges, probation officers,

court-appointed defenders, and special advocates; fund pretrial services (including mental health screening and assessment) for juvenile offenders; establish training programs for law enforcement, court personnel, and juvenile probation officers; create accountability-based programs to reduce recidivism; and establish restorative justice programs.

White Earth Band of Chippewa. The White Earth Reservation is located in northwest Minnesota. The tribe hopes to serve a minimum of 60 juveniles (ages 8 to 17) per year. The goals of the program are to strengthen the reservation's juvenile justice system through increasing the number of hours the associate judge is available in the tribal court, implement a culturally relevant juvenile wellness court to reduce juvenile delinquency and truancy cases, conduct risk and needs assessments (substance abuse and mental health) on all juveniles entering the tribal court for truancy offenses, and provide truant juveniles the opportunity to participate in the Good Path Program, which integrates cultural values and beliefs.

OJJDP Support to the Tribes

OJJDP provides training and technical assistance through a number of providers:

♦ The OJJDP Tribal Youth Training and Technical Assistance Center provides training and technical assistance through e-mails, telephone calls, teleconferences, Web-based discussions, and site visits that address the following:

  ❑ Capacity building.

  ❑ Culturally based approaches to prevention and intervention.

  ❑ Program implementation.

  ❑ Evaluation.

  ❑ Enhancement of tribal court systems.

  ❑ Strategic planning.

  ❑ Sustainability.

- ❏ Youth behavior, including gang membership and youth leadership.

- ◆ CSR, Inc., manages the Data Collection and Technical Assistance Tool that OJJDP encourages tribes to use when submitting JABG performance measurement data. CSR staff also provide training and support to the tribes that use JABG performance measures.

Performance Measurement

In FY 2008, OJJDP had 12 active T–JADG awards, representing $1,130,721 in funding. Of the 12 T–JADG grantees, 6 provided performance data for 2008. Of the 20 grantees during the 2009 reporting period, eight provided performance data. Data for 2008 and 2009 include the following:

- ◆ Sixty-seven percent of programs reported using an evidence-based program or practice (five of six programs) in 2008, and 75 percent of programs reported using an evidence-based program or practice (12 of 16 programs) in 2009.

- ◆ Thirty-one percent of program youth (77 of 246 youth) exhibited a desired change in targeted behavior in 2008, and 59 percent of program youth (504 of 861 youth) exhibited a desired change in targeted behavior in 2009.

- ◆ Eleven percent of program youth (five of 48 youth who exited the program) successfully completed program requirements in 2008, and 74 percent of program youth (110 of 149 youth who exited the program) successfully completed program requirements in 2009.

T–JADG Accomplishments

Healing to Wellness Program—Montana. On the Rocky Boy's Indian Reservation in north central Montana, the Chippewa Cree Tribe is fighting underage drinking through the innovative Healing to Wellness program.

The program helps juveniles recognize and overcome their drinking problem through evaluations, individual treatment plans, and cultural activities designed to build self-esteem. The 9-month Healing to Wellness program partners with a network of agencies that sponsor substance abuse and healthy lifestyle programs. Court sentences are deferred while the youth participate in the program. If a juvenile completes the program, prosecution is deferred.

The program consists of four phases, each of which hold youth accountable for certain actions. In the first phase, youth must attend clinical treatment, appear in court each week, undergo random drug and alcohol testing, and participate in community service. Youth must also be enrolled in school and participate in cultural awareness activities. The second phase emphasizes personal responsibility—youth must meet a curfew, visit with a juvenile court counselor, and participate in drug and alcohol education. In the third phase, the youth assess and apply what they have learned by mentoring other youth in the program and participating in other activities. During the final phase, participants are taught to recognize the signs of relapse, and the number of treatment sessions and random drug and alcohol tests is reduced.

In addition to helping young people overcome alcohol abuse, the Healing to Wellness program has helped reduce the number of repeat offenders. In 1972, the recidivism rate among juveniles on the reservation was 72 percent. By June 2008, that figure had dropped to 24 percent.

The tribe recently expanded the program to include working with parents and providing education and information that fosters the health and well-being of the entire family. The program's goal is to ensure that tribal youth grow up in an environment that predisposes them to success and a healthy way of living.

Chapter 4: Enhancements to OJJDP's Accountability Program

Based on what the Office of Juvenile Justice and Delinquency Prevention (OJJDP) learned through the implementation of the Juvenile Accountability Block Grants (JABG) performance measurement system, experience with the 2006 Juvenile Justice Program Assessment Rating Tool (PART) review, and the appraisal of the JABG 2002 PART results, the Office added a menu of behavior change measures to the JABG system. Exhibit 7 shows these additional mandatory indicators, which went into effect for the sixth data reporting period (April 1, 2008, through March 31, 2009). Preliminary analysis of these performance measures indicates that youth improved in social competency, school attendance, grade point average, General Equivalency Diploma attainment, and family relationships while being involved in the JABG program.

OJJDP is already collecting additional performance measures for several of its other grant programs (the Formula Grants program, the Title V Community Prevention Grants program, the Tribal Youth Program, and its discretionary grants programs). Implementing these measures within the JABG program will help further

Exhibit 7: Mandatory Behavioral Indicators (Effective for Awards Active as of April 1, 2008)

Indicator Type	Direct-Service Programs
Short-term outcome (outcomes realized during the JABG program)	Number and percentage of youth exhibiting the desired change in targeted behaviors: 1. Social competence. 2. School attendance. 3. Grade point average. 4. General Equivalency Diploma. 5. High school graduation. 6. Job skills. 7. Employment status. 8. Teen pregnancy. 9. Family relationships. 10. Antisocial behavior. 11. Substance use. 12. Gang-related activities.

standardize data collection across all of OJJDP's juvenile justice programs.

In addition, OJJDP will continue its contractual relationship with the Bureau of Justice Statistics and the Justice Research and Statistics Association (JRSA). OJJDP anticipates that JRSA will prepare a report on the overall status of the states and how they have implemented JABG. This report will include individual state profiles with information on the purpose areas funded, descriptions of how states and local governments use JABG funds, and information about waiver levels since the performance measurement system was implemented, beginning with the April 2004 data reporting period.

Conclusion

Several broad conclusions can be drawn from the performance data collected and submitted during the fifth and sixth data reporting periods of the Juvenile Accountability Block Grants (JABG) program. First, the JABG performance measurement system has gained acceptance among grantees and subgrantees. Of the 56 states and territories receiving JABG funding, 96 percent submitted performance data during the last reporting period. This growth in the number of grantees who submitted data to the system reflects a growing commitment to and acceptance of this performance measurement initiative.

The JABG data collection system has taught the Office of Juvenile Justice and Delinquency Prevention (OJJDP) how to implement a performance measurement system for a national grant program. This knowledge has informed the agency's approach to implementing performance measurement for other grant programs. The importance of obtaining state buy-in and feedback on the development of the indicators led OJJDP to design and implement the collection system in stages. This staging of the performance measurement process has bought valuable time to conduct training and support state efforts to understand the performance measurement process and promote its adoption among subgrantees. Although staging the process has meant that the pace of implementation has been slow, this additional time is clearly beneficial: an increasing number of states, territories, and subgrantees are building the capacity to collect and report the data needed for the system. OJJDP looks forward to growing, developing, and expanding the data collection across other grant programs within OJJDP.

www.ingramcontent.com/pod-product-compliance
Lightning Source LLC
Chambersburg PA
CBHW080630180526
45168CB00007B/3109